Transportation

LIFE IN AMERICA 100 YEARS AGO

Transportation

Linda Leuzzi

Chelsea House Publishers

New York   Philadelphia

S

CHELSEA HOUSE PUBLISHERS

Editorial Director: Richard Rennert
Executive Managing Editor: Karyn Gullen Browne
Copy Chief: Robin James
Picture Editor: Adrian G. Allen
Art Director: Robert Mitchell
Manufacturing Director: Gerald Levine
Assistant Art Director: Joan Ferrigno

LIFE IN AMERICA 100 YEARS AGO
Senior Editor: Jake Goldberg

Staff for **TRANSPORTATION**
Assistant Editor: Annie McDonnell
Designer: Lydia Rivera
Picture Researcher: Sandy Jones
Cover Illustrator: Steve Cieslawski

First Printing

1   3   5   7   9   8   6   4   2

Library of Congress Cataloging-in-Publication Data

Leuzzi, Linda.
    Transportation/Linda Leuzzi.
        p. cm.—(Life 100 years ago)
    Includes bibliographical references and index.
    ISBN 0-7910-2840-2
    Transportation—United States—History—19th century—Juvenile literature.
[1. Transportation—History.] I. Title. II. Series.
HE204.L4 1994
388—dc20

94-17183
CIP
AC

CONTENTS

LIFE IN AMERICA 100 YEARS AGO

Health and Medicine

Law and Order

Manners and Customs

Rural Life

Transportation

Urban Life

Transportation

The Beginnings of American Transportation

IMAGINE ARRIVING IN A NEW LAND WHERE OAK, PINE, juniper, and sassafras trees grow down to the water's edge. This new place has sandhills, rocky places, scrub, and swamps surrounded by cedar trees and red maples. There is no town, no inn, and no home where horses can be bought or borrowed. A vast ocean hugs the coastline and, because of the thick forests, provides the only practical way to get around.

This is what the first English colonists faced when they arrived in North America, after traveling the Atlantic Ocean for more than 60 days. Back then, the only practical roads between settlements were the waterways, and the ocean was the sole connection to supplies from England and markets for colonial products. The first settlers had few vessels. Some had small boats from the ships that had brought them across the ocean and canoes obtained through barter with nearby Native Americans, but this was not enough. Boats were needed to travel along the coast and up the local rivers, where new land could be found and new communities established.

Around 1890, just about anyone—farmer, clergyman, doctor, or tradesman—who needed a horse to get around owned a fast trotter and a carriage like the one in this picture. By the turn of the century, there were 21 million horses in the United States and only about 4,000 automobiles. While it seemed unlikely at the time, Americans would end their dependence on the horse within the next quarter century.

Almost every colony quickly sent home to England for skilled boatbuilders and shipwrights. As these craftsmen came, the construction of small boats for fishing and transportation began. Small boats were used much as the family pickup truck is used today, and eventually, most boatmen learned to build their own vessels.

The early settlers' connection to the ocean remained solid for more than a hundred years after the *Mayflower* landed. Busy seaports developed along the eastern American coastline. In New England, there was Portsmouth, Boston, Salem, Bristol, and Newport, which thrived on shipbuilding, cod and mackerel fishing, and the export trade with the Orient. New York was famous for its beaver skin and

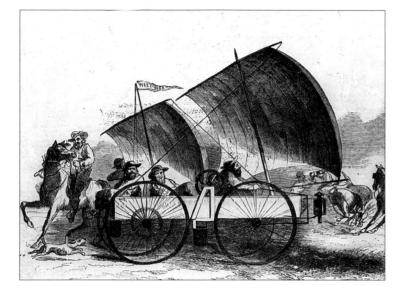

An 1860 windship. Windships were often designed to run on railroad tracks, as was the *Meteour*, invented by Evan Thomas, which ran on the Baltimore & Ohio Railroad. In 1830, the *Charleston Courier* reported that a windship similar to the *Meteour* carried 13 people and three tons of iron at about 10 miles per hour. The car had a mast and rigging and a crew to maneuver the sail.

flour exports; Philadelphia for its pottery, tannery supplies, silverware, pewter, and brass buttons; Baltimore for its shipbuilding, and later, coffee and wheat exports. In the South, Charleston, Savannah, and New Orleans exported rice, indigo, deer skins, liquor, livestock, sugar, and cotton.

In the years before the American Revolution, settlers who tried to branch out and cross the physically imposing Appalachians to make their homes in the Ohio, Missouri, and Mississippi river valleys were discouraged by what lay before them. The Appalachians were 120 to 325 miles wide, and the Native Americans who lived to the west were hostile. It was not until the late 18th century that increasing numbers of Americans crossed the Alleghenies, the central Appalachian mountain range that provided the most manageable route west.

A United States mail coach that operated out of Sharon Springs, New York. The entire West, as well as Vermont, Kentucky, and Tennessee, lacked post offices as late as the 1790s. That changed in 1794, when an act of Congress was passed mandating the construction of more post roads and stagecoach transportation. By the 1830s, there were more than 100,000 miles of post roads. The basic postal rate was 6 cents up to 30 miles, 10 cents up to 80 miles, and 25 cents over 400 miles. Private companies were often given contracts for mail service in the far western regions of the country.

A horse-drawn bus. America's earliest form of mass transportation was the omnibus, invented by Abraham Brower. Brower offered a horse-drawn, multiple-passenger service between Broadway and Bleecker Street in New York City. Omnibus fleets appeared in Philadelphia in 1831, Boston by 1835, and Baltimore by 1844. These buses moved people from one part of the city to another, from their homes to offices, shops, and schools. As populations grew, cities were challenged to develop faster forms of commuting.

TROY, BALLSTON AND SARATOGA,

DAILY LINE OF COACHES.

This line will commence running on the first day of July, leaving each place at half past 8 A. M. every day. Passengers wishing to travel from Saratoga to Lebanon Springs, will find this line not only the most expeditious but cheapest.

Passengers for Pittsfield, Northampton and Hartford by taking this line will dine at Troy, lodge at Pittsfield, and arrive at Hartford early the next day. The road is now put in the best order, and all that is now wanting is that liberality which the establishment merits.

☞ *Seats taken at G. W. Wilcox's, York House, Saratoga,* and at all the Principal Houses in Troy.

L. V. & J. B. REED, Proprietors.
J. S. KEELER, *Agent,* Troy.
S. DEXTER, *Agent,* Saratoga.

TROY, JUNE 25, 1834.

N. B. On the arrival of the **ERIE** or **CHAMPLAIN**, Parties can be accommodated with coaches to Saratoga or Ballston the same evening.

An 1834 advertisement for the Troy Saratoga stagecoach line. Stagecoaches began to appear in the West around 1820, and with them coach stations positioned strategically along the dusty trails of the frontier. Many new companies appeared, like the California Stage Company, which offered daily service over most of its lines. By the 1860s, the company had 1,000 horses and 134 coaches to service its customers and ran 28 stage lines over nearly 2,000 miles of California territory.

Winding through southern Pennsylvania and the Potomac River valley, the Allegheny route became the main trail for most settlers traveling by horse and wagon.

As frontier communities formed, agricultural crops grown for eastern markets were sent downstream on rafts or boats, eventually reaching New Orleans and other gulf towns. Ships then carried these goods to eastern or foreign cities. Overland travel was difficult, expensive, and dangerous. But as roads and trails improved, the horse and wagon were used to haul farm goods east and manufactured goods west. These wagon teams jostled over the mountains on dangerous, narrow roads to western rivers, where goods were floated to a river town and hauled overland to their final destination.

The famous Conestoga wagons were designed specifically to withstand these rough-and-tumble journeys. Manufactured in southeastern Pennsylvania, these sturdy wagons hauled freight and crops over dusty and muddy dirt roads. Americans would build other sturdy freight wagons, but all were fashioned after the Conestoga.

Some decent roads helped tame these bumpy trips somewhat. The road from Philadelphia leading to Lancaster and the western lands beyond, begun in 1792 by the Philadelphia and Lancaster Turnpike Company, became the country's first turnpike. Used in the early 19th century by farmers, emigrants, freighters, and others, the traffic became so heavy right after the revolutionary war that a better road became necessary.

Wagons loaded with merchandise, sometimes weighing 3,500 pounds, also lumbered down the National Road, or Cumberland Road, which connected Cumberland and Baltimore, Maryland, with Wheeling, Virginia (now in West Virginia). The road had been built to accommodate the heavy trade that had developed between the western ports of Pittsburgh and Wheeling, on the Ohio River, and the old eastern seaboard cities of Philadelphia and Baltimore. The Ohio valley became so important after the Revolution that a good road was needed to serve the southern states. Construction for the National Road began in 1811 at Cumberland and reached Wheeling in 1818.

But even with a smoother ride, it took a wagoner about 15 days, averaging 15 miles a day, to travel the 226 miles from Wheeling to

A coaching party of the well-to-do leaving their home in Newport, Rhode Island. The demand for small carriages reached its peak by 1850, when there were more than one thousand carriage builders in the country. The work of construction was slow and painstaking, and the average cost of a good carriage was $500. Jacob Huntington of Massachusetts revolutionized the industry by mass producing interchangeable carriage parts in his Cincinnati factory, reducing the cost of a good carriage to between $50 and $100. In wealthy areas like Newport, the carriage was used as a way to show off the latest fashions and to make social rounds. In the late 1880s, between 4 P.M. and dusk, carriages would crowd Newport's beautiful Bellevue Avenue. By 1905, the carriage industry had been almost destroyed by the automobile, but as late as 1935 there were still about 3,000 buggies manufactured each year for use in rural areas. In Lancaster, Pennsylvania, the Amish still make carriages for their communities.

A Hansom cab in front of a New York hotel around 1900. In a study of New York traffic undertaken in 1907, horse-drawn vehicles moved at an average speed of 11.5 miles per hour. In a similar study conducted almost 60 years later, it was found that automobiles moved through the city's business district at an average speed of only 8.5 miles per hour.

Baltimore. Because moving goods was difficult and expensive, westerners formed self-sufficient towns that had a number of manufacturing businesses. They processed their own agricultural goods, sawed wood, spun thread and wove cloth, and produced and repaired machinery and household items.

Rolling prairies, parched deserts, and towering mountains made their gritty stamp on most of the Old West, but the territory was also blessed with thousands of miles of navigable rivers. The successful trip of Robert Fulton's steamboat—a paddleboat powered by steam that traveled on the Hudson River from New York City to Albany and back in 1807—introduced a new kind of transportation. Fulton's invention, which hauled freight, animals, and people along the rivers of the Old West, helped lessen the isolation of the region soon after the 1830s.

Steamers from the Pacific coast churned hundreds of miles eastward on the Columbia and Sacramento rivers and their tributaries, making their way along the Colorado River, the waters of Puget Sound in Washington Territory, and the Snohomish and the Skagit, shorter rivers that flowed into Puget Sound. Steamers navigating the Missouri, where it merges with the Mississippi, moved into the Dakotas and Montana. Other steamers turned off the Missouri at the mouth of the Yellowstone, forging up that river for nearly 483 miles to within 60 miles of Yellowstone National Park. These steamers could carry 400 tons of freight and 200 passengers.

But there were still areas that the rivers did not penetrate. The lack of efficient transportation that could link these areas to more prosperous regions held back economic growth and development. Developers began looking at canal systems.

France had already built the Canal of Languedoc, connecting the Atlantic with the Mediterranean, and Great Britain had its own canal system in the late 18th and early 19th centuries. A canal plan originally reviewed by the federal government was funded by the state of New York, and the Erie Canal—a 353-mile-long waterway with 77 locks and a total rise and fall of 661 feet—was begun in 1817, connecting the Hudson River to Lake Erie through upstate New York. It opened in 1825, and its success sparked a new type of transportation access to the interior. By 1840, over 3,000 miles of these artificial waterways had been built. In Ohio and Indiana, for example, a shipment of goods could travel south to the Ohio River. From the Ohio, a riverboat would then transport the goods down the Mississippi to the Gulf of Mexico; or the freight could head north to the Great Lakes and through the Erie Canal to New York City.

Until the Central Pacific Railroad was completed in 1869, however, there were only three basic means for settlers and freight haulers to travel from the East to the West Coast. Overland, with the help of animals, was one way. Oxen, horses, or mules, grunting and tugging in caravans ranging from two to over a hundred rumbling wagons and stagecoaches, trudged over nearly 2,000 miles of sparsely inhabited territory that lay between Missouri River outposts such as St. Joseph and Independence, and western coastal cities such as Sacramento.

Wagon trains jostled along the rough dirt tracks of the Overland Trail, primarily an emigrant road, and the Santa Fe Trail, used more as a commercial road. These two main westward systems had various branches. For example, the Overland Trail included the Oregon Trail, the Mormon Trail, the California Trail, and the Bozeman Trail. These trails followed rivers; crossed plains, mountains, and deserts; and

An 1832 illustration of the Erie Canal. The Erie Canal, or the Grand Canal as it was then called, ran for more than 360 miles from the Hudson River to Lake Erie and had a major impact on the nation's commerce. By 1850, the canal was carrying 23 million bushels of wheat and flour, representing 25 percent of the nation's entire grain production. With the canal, trade with the western states increased more than 500 percent.

Streetcars pulled on tracks by horses were in some cities before the Civil War. Streetcars drawn by sixteen-horse teams were operating in New York City by 1866. Because of the large volumes of hay consumed by the horses, the cars were known as hayburners. Caring for the animals was expensive and difficult. Owners feared another outbreak of the "Great Epizootic," the terrible epidemic that killed thousands of trolley horses in 1872. Electric streetcars became a reality when Frank Sprague built a 12-mile electric trolley line in Richmond, Virginia, in 1888.

went skyward in elevation. By 1852, over 100,000 people had used the Overland Trail to reach California.

The remaining two routes to the West Coast were by sea. The first route went south to the Isthmus of Panama in Central America, across the isthmus to the sea again, and finally by boat to California.

The second way was the 17,000-mile journey south around Cape Horn at the tip of South America. The Cape Horn route could be easily attempted during winter—a big advantage over the land trips, because the trails were almost impossible to traverse in cold months. Also, freight could be transported much more cheaply on the Cape

Horn route; hauling goods through the tropical jungle made the Panama run expensive.

While it was less costly than the Panama route, the cape journey was not easy. Ships making the journey between New York and California battled the weather conditions of both the tropics and the Antarctic. The discovery of gold in California, and the resulting flood of emigrants to that part of the country, created a big demand for consumer goods in San Francisco. For ship owners, developing a speedy vessel became the key to big profits. American clipper ships, the fastest windjammers ever built, were designed to skim over the waves. They "clipped" off the miles and were larger and stronger than any other sailing ships.

While clippers mainly hauled freight, steamers bound for the Panama route carried most of the passengers who headed for the West by sea. The Panama route was chosen by the government as the most practical mail route to Oregon in 1846; it was also an important travel and communication link between California and the East Coast from 1848 to 1869.

But railroads soon rendered sea travel unnecessary. Sea routes could take up to six months. But locomotives could operate in any season and scale hills and mountains easily. And they could venture into areas canals could not reach. The first railroads were backed by municipal governments and enterprising businessmen. These trains initially chugged short distances inland to explore potential markets. But by 1860, most major cities and towns were connected by more than 30,000 miles of tracks.

In 1862, the Pacific Railroad Act was passed, authorizing the Union Pacific Railroad to build westward from Omaha, and the Central Pacific Railroad to build eastward from Sacramento. On January 8,

An early stone marker. When the first colonists came, there were no roads, only a few Indian trails. Dirt roads were an improvement, but the revolution in transportation began with roads like the National Road, also called the Cumberland Road, a paved highway connecting Cumberland, Maryland, with Wheeling, West Virginia, and Columbus, Ohio, and ending at Vandalia, Illinois.

1863, the Central Pacific Railroad broke ground at Sacramento. Six years later, locomotives of the two railroads met at Promontory, Utah. By 1885, most of the Old West had been linked by rail.

Economically, the railroads were a major influence that helped turn the country into a prominent industrial power by the 20th century. The growth of cities also helped. After 1875, new immigrants looking for a better life flocked to bustling urban areas, creating huge

A traffic jam at Randolph and Dearborn streets in Chicago in 1905. Traffic jams were common in industrial cities like Chicago, where horse-drawn vehicles, electric streetcars, and pedestrians competed for space. The old downtown sections of cities were too narrow for heavy traffic; some of the streets had cobblestone surfaces, but most were dirt, which turned to mud or dust depending on the weather. Many cities paved their streets with wooden blocks, bricks, or asphalt by the end of the 19th century.

demands for food, clothing, and new products, and by the end of the century, 40 percent of the American population lived in cities.

Railroads moved the goods that consumers in these urban areas demanded. Trains carried wheat, corn, and hogs from the Great Plains, cotton from the Mississippi Delta, lumber from Wisconsin and the Northwest, oil products from Pennsylvania, and coal from West Virginia and Kentucky. In the West, railroads sold settlers the land granted to them by the federal government. Towns along railroad routes prospered. By the end of the 19th century, when refrigerated cars were carrying meats, fruits, and vegetables, there were five transcontinental railroads serving the United States.

New technology also pushed the economy forward. Thomas Edison introduced the filament lightbulb in 1879, and electricity was soon to become a major source of power. By 1890, there were 25,000 annual patent applications, and the inventions that emerged changed the face of the country. The Bessemer converter, invented in England by Sir Henry Bessemer, improved the quality and quantity of steel production and helped to supply the railroad with rails, frames, wheels, and other machinery.

Americans had become a mobile society and, at the turn of the century, began to abandon their horses and buggies for horseless carriages that ran on refined petroleum.

Politically, events were changing the country's isolationist attitudes. Britain, France, Germany, and Russia were establishing colonies in Asia and Africa during the last quarter of the 19th century. Captain Alfred Thayer Mahan, a naval strategist who spent most of his career observing European politics firsthand, wrote a book urging the United States to become more expansionist in its foreign policy. Mahan believed that establishing naval supremacy, controlling the world's sea lanes, and developing foreign markets were necessary to make the United States a great power. That meant more ships.

A number of international disputes in the 1890s seemed to support Mahan's arguments. Some of them were relatively minor, but in 1897, the American battleship *Maine* was destroyed in Havana harbor. Cuba was still under Spain's rule at that time, but not peaceably. After the *Maine* uproar, President McKinley made several demands of Spain, the most important being Cuba's independence. By the time Spain partially agreed, it was too late, and war was declared on April 19, 1898. The war was short. Spain's navy was no match for American naval squadrons. A few months after war had been declared in 1898, Spain relinquished Cuba, the Philippines, Puerto Rico, and Guam.

Theodore Roosevelt, who agreed with Captain Mahan's aggressive foreign policy for the United States, became president in 1901 after McKinley's assassination. Roosevelt intervened many times in the domestic affairs of his Caribbean neighbors, adopting the role of policeman under the guise of protecting their independence. His policies smoothed the way for American companies who wanted to do business in these countries.

Most significantly, in 1903, Roosevelt pushed for and obtained a canal route through Panama by sending the U.S. Navy to back a revolution that gave Panama independence from Colombia. The new state of Panama gave the United States a six-mile canal zone for a reasonable $10 million and an annual rental fee of $250,000—the same terms the Colombians had refused.

Steamboats and Steamships

THE YEAR WAS 1807. IT WAS A STRANGE-LOOKING BOAT. It was 140 feet long with waterwheels 15 feet in diameter on each side. Its machinery and paddles made a lot of noise, and a column of vapor billowed up from the flue. Whenever the dry pinewood fuel was stirred, sparks flew up, lighting up the night sky. It looked, some said, like a monster moving on the waters, defying the wind and tide.

This was Robert Fulton's *North River Steamboat,* or the *Clermont.* It took 32 hours to sail the 150-mile trial trip from a dock in New York City to Albany, and 30 hours to return. Fulton was not the first in the United States to develop a vessel powered by steam. A man named John Fitch of Connecticut sailed a trial steam vessel in 1787. But Fulton was able to join his mechanical skill with financial backing by teaming up with Robert R. Livingston, a wealthy man who was also an inventor. Fulton's ability to place the machinery in the vessel so that it floated on an even keel—not an easy task even for today's boatbuilders—made his the first successful steamboat in the world.

An old windjammer under full sail in 1910. Sailing vessels continued to be an economical way of transporting goods well into the 20th century. Warships and large passenger ships used steam and later diesel power, but as late as 1907 about 40 percent of the commercial vessels used in North America were sailing ships like this one.

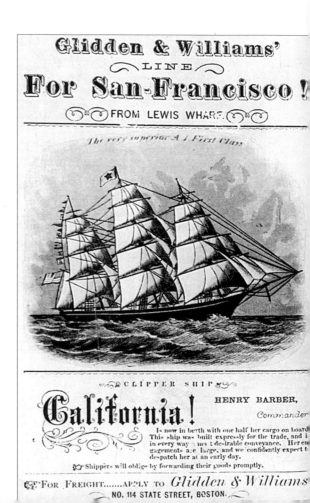

Glidden & Williams' LINE
For San-Francisco!
FROM LEWIS WHARF.

The very superior A 1 First Class

CLIPPER SHIP

California!

HENRY BARBER, *Commander*

Is now in berth with one half her cargo on board. This ship was built expressly for the trade, and i in every way a most desirable conveyance. Her engagements are large, and we confidently expect to despatch her at an early day.

Shippers will oblige by forwarding their goods promptly.

FOR FREIGHT......APPLY TO *Glidden & Williams,*
NO. 114 STATE STREET, BOSTON.

An 1873 advertisement for the clipper *California*. Clippers were dubbed "moonrakers" because of their beautiful, towering, wooden masts. These striking vessels, with their large sails, long, lean hulls, and knifelike prows, seemed to clip the waves in full sail. About 500 of these ships were built during the 1840s and '50s. They were fast and cheaper to build than steamships. The income from one load of cargo could pay the vessel's purchase price in one voyage. Originally built to carry tea and spices from the Orient, they also transported forty-niners to the West Coast during California's gold rush.

Fulton's steamboat, which began taking passengers two weeks after its trial run, was an instant hit. Passengers were willing to pay seven dollars for the trip, an expensive fare in those times. Fulton's boats had masts and sails, as did most early steamboats, with a flush main deck and an awning for passengers to stand under.

The dense forests on the banks of rivers supplied a virtually free and unlimited fuel supply for the steamboats, and in 1811 the *New Orleans* was the first boat to steam down the Ohio and Mississippi rivers. Steamboats became the new means of travel to and through the West via its rivers.

The Mississippi River starts in Minnesota and runs all the way to the Gulf of Mexico. The Ohio River originates in Pittsburgh, Pennsylvania, and flows many miles to connect with the Mississippi at Cairo, Illinois. Henry Miller Shreve, an expert keelboat and flatboat captain, knew the changeable conditions of the Ohio and Mississippi rivers like the back of his hand. He built his own steamboat, the *Washington,* a double-decker with a trusslike arrangement of heavy timbers called a hogging frame, and a flat, shallow hull—as opposed to Fulton's deep, round hull—which would help glide the boat over low water. It successfully went through the falls of the Ohio River in 1816 and proceeded to New Orleans.

Shreve, who eventually owned or partly owned the first 60 steamboats on these rivers, successfully fought against Fulton and Livingston in their attempts to monopolize the western waterways. He even cleared thousands of partially sunken dead trees, called snags, along a 300-mile stretch of the Mississippi. Shreve's innovations were adopted by other western steamboat builders, and by 1842, 450 boats were transporting people and goods on the Mississippi and the Ohio. Shreveport, Louisiana, was eventually

29

The Mississippi River steamboat *Natchez* was one of the most famous steamboats of its day, the other being the *Robert E. Lee*. Tom Leathers, owner of the *Natchez*, was an arrogant but skillful river skipper who worked the lucrative Vicksburg to New Orleans run for 35 years. He loved the city of Natchez and named seven boats after it. When John Cannon, skipper of the *Robert E. Lee*, extended his passenger route to cover the same cities, Leathers felt that it was an invasion of his market. The two men became heated rivals and engaged in one of the greatest steamboat races of the time in 1870. The *Robert E. Lee* won the 1,200-mile race between New Orleans and St. Louis on July 4, taking 3 days, 18 hours, and 14 minutes. The *Natchez* pulled in 7 hours later. True to his temperament, Leathers refused to concede defeat, or even that there had been a race.

named after Shreve, in honor of his efforts to open up the rivers he loved.

As Shreve adapted his steamboat, others varied theirs, too. While some vessels had side paddle wheels, other steamboats had stern wheels, at the rear part of the boat. Steamers on the upper Missouri River were called mountain boats and were smaller and lighter than the Mississippi boats. But all steamboats had decks above the hull, the ship's body, and they were almost always painted white.

The steamboat became an important part of life for the river towns. Most of the residents would wander down to the landing when a steamboat announced its arrival with a whistle blast, looking to see who arrived and what the latest news was. If there was a band, the townspeople could come on board and dance, and they could even have a meal. The captain would make arrangements for fuel, freight would be picked up and delivered, and passengers could leave or embark.

The earlier steamboats were far from luxurious, but later on, passenger steamboats developed into graceful, beautiful vessels. Some, like the night boats on the Hudson River and Long Island Sound in the 1870s, had two-story grand salons where passengers could walk on plush carpets and gaze over the upper-level rails. Sleeping quarters, called staterooms, opened onto the salons. Comfortable armchairs were placed here and there for reading or observing, and there were tables on the main level.

The floating palaces of the Mississippi displayed large mirrors to make their interiors look even bigger. Artisans carved the beautiful woodwork on walls and moldings, and Belgian weavers painstakingly created the floral designs in the carpets. Huge

TRANSPORTATION

Unloading a paddle wheeler on the Mississippi. River towns and steamboats needed each other. When a steamboat pulled into a town landing, the area came to life. Passengers and cargo handlers bustled about and wood, used as fuel, was loaded aboard. On larger boats, the passengers might be rich cotton planters, lawyers, and politicians, as well as gamblers and prostitutes. Some of the boats had small brass bands or orchestras, which drew the townspeople down to the landing to listen and dance.

A scene on the levee at New Orleans in 1881, revealing how important a center of commerce the city had become.

gilt-painted pillars and arches reflected the golden light that came from the crystal chandeliers.

Eight hundred steamboats were on the western rivers by the time of the Civil War. They were used by Union and Confederate commanders for transporting troops and supplies and for assaults

33

Steamboats docked along a Mississippi landing near Nashville, Tennessee, in the late 1870s. During the Civil War, steamboats were pressed into service by Union and Confederate armies to carry soldiers and supplies. One boat might carry as many as 2,500 soldiers.

against riverside forts. These steamboats were called ironclads because of the plates of metal that covered their main frame.

Steamships had been sailing along the Atlantic coast since their appearance. While the steamship was basically the offspring of the steamboat, the major difference was the location of the engines. Steamships had their machinery located in the interior of the ship, while steamboats had theirs located on the deck.

The sidewheeler *Pilgrim* of the Fall River Line in 1883. Founded in 1846 by Fall River and Boston investors, the Fall River Line began with two steamers that ran between Fall River and New York City. Competition for steamboat passengers was intense among the lines running on Long Island Sound in the 1860s. Companies added sleeping accommodations and money was spent generously on decoration. The *Pilgrim* was the Fall River Line's first iron-hull vessel. It could accommodate 675 passengers.

The *Commonwealth,* another Fall River Line steamer. The Fall River Line was famous for its big steamships; they were called the Queens of the Sound.

The first steamship to cross the Atlantic was called the *Savannah*. Built in New York City in 1818, it was 100 feet long and had wrought-iron waterwheels that were 16 feet in diameter. The steamship left Savannah, Georgia, on May 24, 1819, and arrived in Liverpool, England, 27 days later. It was an auxiliary steamship, which meant it relied on its sails at times, but steam power was used for 80 hours of the journey. The steamship had a successful voyage, stopping at

The dining salon of the steamer *Victoria* in 1902. When not used for meals, the salon could be set up for use as a lounge, writing room, or concert hall.

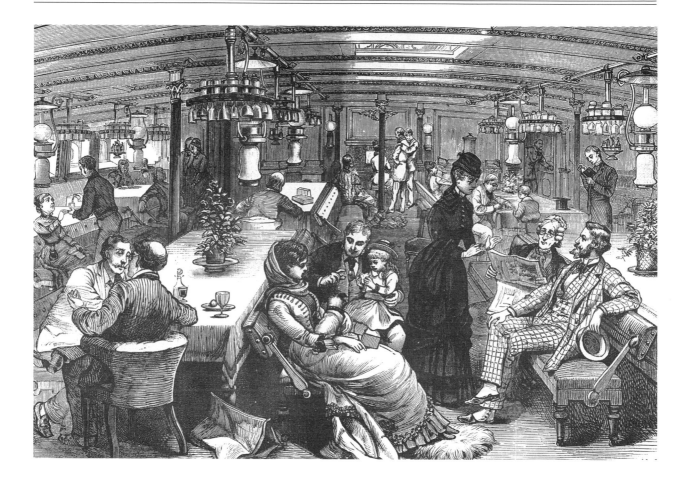

The salon of the Inman Line's *City of Chester*. The Inman line became prosperous by transporting more than half a million immigrants to America. It was the first steamship line to offer passage at a cheap fare with decent, nutritious food and bathing facilities. Some of the line's steamers offered large private suites, brass beds, sitting rooms, and toilets with baths. Dining rooms had glass ceilings and little alcoves where private dinner parties could be held.

A ferryboat on the Mississippi near New Orleans, Louisiana. While the scene here looks peaceful, steamboat travel had its dangers. There were boiler explosions and fires, groundings during fog and storms, and collisions with ice and fallen trees. Between 1865 and 1910, there were more than 2,500 riverboat accidents.

St. Petersburg and Kronstadt in Russia, and at Stockholm, Sweden, and some other Baltic ports. But because so much room had to be used for the machinery, there was very little space for revenue-producing cargo. The *Savannah*'s machinery was dismantled and sold, and its hull was converted into a sailing vessel shortly after its return. It was a long time before another steamship owned by an American company crossed the Atlantic.

In 1847, the Oceanic Steam Navigation Company offered America's first transatlantic steamship for service, the *Washington*. The

Washington's competition was the *Britannia,* a luxury steamship launched by Great Britain's Cunard Line in 1840. The *Britannia* sailed to Southampton, England, from the United States on the same day as the *Washington* and beat the American vessel by two days. But the *Washington* provided regular passenger service for several years, and its arrival sparked a passenger liner competition that became intense.

In 1850, the Collins Line introduced the *Atlantic,* a steamship with an opulent salon; light, airy staterooms; and marble tabletops. It was also bigger than the *Britannia.* Founded in 1847, the Collins Line had a reputation for luxurious accommodations and fast service. The U.S. government even gave the company a contract for overseas mail service, but because of its extravagant interiors and services, and the expensive maintenance required after each voyage, the Collins Line never made a profit.

Paddle wheels were efficient in the rivers and in shallow water, but they were not effective for ocean liners, especially in rough seas. A lot of coal had to be used to travel short distances, and the massive weight of the paddle wheels and their pistons imposed great stresses on the boat. John Ericsson, a Swedish engineer, patented a screw propeller in the United States in 1837. The screw propeller provided more thrust per horsepower, but the design weakened the hull, which was made of wood and invariably leaked.

Sir Isambard Brunel of Great Britain, who conducted the first steam-powered propeller experiments with American John Stevens on the Passaic River, built the first transatlantic steamship with a screw propeller in 1843. The *Pioneer* and the *City of Pittsburgh* were the first American propeller-driven steamships to cross the Atlantic, in 1851.

The *Olympic* leaves Southampton, England, in 1912. The White Star Line set out to build the biggest and most luxurious liners for transatlantic service and met its goal in 1911 with the launching of the *Olympic,* the largest ship of its time. The *Olympic* had an indoor swimming pool, bronze lamps, and marble drinking fountains. There were 1,054 first-class berths and 510 second-class berths, with room for 1,020 more passengers, mostly immigrants, in third class.

Several important developments turned steamships into big business. Iron ships could withstand the stresses of the screw propeller, but it was not until the large-scale production of iron began that iron vessels could become a reality. In the 1860s, a compound engine was introduced that was smaller and operated on half the fuel, which meant less coal storage and more space to carry cargo. The compound engine kicked off a boom in steamship construction. The introduction of twin-screw propulsion and the use of steel were other technological triumphs that fostered the steamships' glory days from 1870 to 1950.

Until the development of twin-screw propulsion, all steamships were outfitted with sails. They were used as auxiliary power, in case of engine failure. But with two shafts providing the power, the graceful sails and masts became unnecessary. Once the sails were removed, the shape of the steamship changed. A tier-on-tier form emerged, which was high in the middle and low on the ends. Decks had open railings around the perimeters, and decks stacked above provided overhead protection.

The *City of Paris* and the *City of New York* were the first American twin-screw sister ships. They were also the last clipper-bowed deluxe liners built for the Atlantic. They had watertight compartments and bulkheads. Both were used as merchant cruisers during the Spanish-American War. The *City of Paris* steamed more than 270,000 miles during World War I and carried 30,000 troops to France.

The largest ocean liner of its time was the *Olympic,* a 45,000-ton luxury liner launched in 1911 by the White Star Line, a British firm eventually taken over by the American industrialist J. Pierpont Morgan. The *Olympic* had four towering smokestacks, the first indoor swimming pool on any liner, and a lush greenhouse area called the

A well-to-do couple takes a stroll on the deck of the *Teutonic* in 1894.

Palm Court. There were 1,054 first-class, 510 second-class, and 1,020 third-class berths. European immigrants were now coming to America in large numbers, and the White Star Line's biggest profits would come from the immigrants who booked these third-class quarters to the States.

The Railroads

RAILROAD SUPERVISION BY THE EASTERN STATES BEFORE
the Civil War had been fairly lax. Among the minor concerns were
checking the tally on interstate receipts and, for the more religious
citizens, the moral debate about running trains on Sunday. Because
of rate wars, there were no established rates for eastern shippers
and merchants, and the railroads changed their fares as often as
50 times or more in one year, disrupting business. But when farming
and crop production shifted westward with the completion of
the first transcontinental railroad in 1869, railroad abuses became
more serious.

For one thing, western railroad freight rates were higher than those
of the eastern railroad companies. Illinois, Missouri, Kansas,
Colorado, Utah, Nevada, California, Oregon, and Washington were
served by four rail lines originating in Chicago. From 1866 to 1870,
these lines charged from 2.2 cents to 2.5 cents per ton-mile from
Chicago to the Missouri River, while several companies east of
Chicago charged average rates of 1.25 cents to 1.6 cents per ton-mile.

The parts for this John Bull Locomotive were made in England and shipped to America, where it was assembled in 1832. The British were the first to build successful steam locomotives. In 1698, Thomas Savery used a steam engine to pump water out of a coal mine. The mechanic Richard Trevethick built a small steam engine with a controllable throttle and attached it to a horseless wagon, which he drove through southwest England in 1800. In 1825, George Stephenson built a steam locomotive that pulled 30 cars loaded with freight at 8 miles per hour. Five years later the Liverpool and Manchester Railway, the first steam-powered rail service in the world, opened in England. The John Bull locomotive was a Stephenson design.

The western farmer also had a longer haul, an average of 201 miles in seven northwestern states versus the national average of 113 miles. On top of that, free travel passes liberally distributed to public officials by the railroad companies to secure favorable legislation were outrageous not only to the farmer, but to everyone else who had to pay the full fare.

Farmers united and gained political power. In 1867, Oliver H. Kelley, a former Minnesota farmer who worked for the Bureau of Agriculture, founded the National Grange of the Patrons of Husbandry. He eventually left his post to establish local Granges for the new organization, and in 1871, the Grangers pushed for and obtained the first significant railroad regulation at the state level, in Illinois. The legislation established maximum passenger fares and uniform freight rates based on distance. Iowa and Wisconsin passed Granger railroad legislation in 1874, and Nebraska, Kansas, and Missouri followed by the end of the decade. By 1875, Kelley's

A later reconstruction of one of the first steam-powered trains used by the Baltimore and Ohio Railroad in 1832, with passenger cars modeled after the stagecoach. The company was founded by Boston merchants in 1827 and tested its first steam locomotive, the *Tom Thumb*, in 1830.

organization had grown to 20,000 local Grange organizations and 800,000 members.

The railroads fought back and won some minor appeals, but in 1876, the U.S. Supreme Court ruled in favor of the Grange members and public regulation of the railroads. In a series of decisions, the Court upheld an Illinois law of 1871 fixing maximum rates for grain storage. It also decreed that besides establishing set passenger and freight rates, states could apply this regulation to interstate commerce.

By the 1880s, railroads were becoming too unwieldy for the states to regulate because of mergers, takeovers, and various monopolistic practices. The federal government, concerned about railroad abuses, initiated an investigation, and a special Senate committee was formed. In 1886, the Cullom Committee cited a number of unfair practices, including arbitrary fares, secret rebates, and wasteful management. The committee suggested forming an independent commission to regulate the railroads nationally. That same year, the Supreme Court reversed its decision about interstate commerce: states could not regulate rates on shipments traveling outside their borders; that was the federal government's job. To address these issues, the Interstate Commerce Act was passed in 1887.

The Interstate Commerce Act attempted to get tough with the railroads. It required published rate schedules in every depot, and these schedules had to be filed with the government. Higher rates for noncompetitive short hauls were against the law, as were secret rebates and other unsavory practices. And rates had to be reasonable and just. Five men were appointed to enforce the act and to review complaints. The commission could demand annual reports from the railroads and review their books and records.

(continued on page 53)

A Currier and Ives lithograph of the trains of the Erie Railroad.

An express train en route is pictured in this 1850 lithograph.

A paddlewheel boat race on the Mississippi in 1871. Although paddlewheelers were already in decline before the Civil War, as late as 1880 more than 300 such steamers still worked the river.

The New York ferry *Fulton,* owned by the Union Ferry Company, traveled on New York's East River. Before steam propulsion, it was virtually impossible to maneuver in the East and Hudson rivers during winter, when masses of floating ice could crush a small vessel's hull. As a result, the boroughs of Brooklyn and Manhattan were often isolated for days.

(*continued from page 48*)

The commission appointees were capable men. All had legal training and several had experience dealing with railroad problems. But terms such as "reasonable and just rates" were vague and caused difficulties. Investigating rate abuse was a long and complicated process, and when final decisions were made, railroads often ignored them. Appeals of the commission's decisions slowed down any court action that might be taken against the railroads.

The effectiveness of the Interstate Commerce Commission, which started out in concept as a powerful regulatory tool, unraveled with two Supreme Court decisions in 1897 and 1901. The Court held that the commission had no jurisdiction over rate making, nor could it prohibit higher charges for shorter hauls. The Sherman Anti-Trust Act, passed in 1890 to stop railroad mergers, shared a similar fate. The act mentioned the illegality of "unreasonable restraint" of trade but did not specify what that term meant or how the government could effectively break up these trusts.

The Sherman Anti-Trust Act did score a major victory in 1904 when it dashed J. P. Morgan's dream of consolidating the Northern Pacific, Union Pacific, and Burlington railroads. But by 1906, the numerous independent systems that had thrived in the early 1890s had been gobbled up. Seven railroads groups controlled nearly two-thirds of the nation's rail lines. Financial manipulations to achieve these mergers were often corrupt and unscrupulous, with inside investors pocketing private profits.

The administrations of Grover Cleveland and William McKinley favored railroad consolidation, but President Theodore Roosevelt championed stricter regulations. He secured from Congress the Expedition Act of 1903. This legislation sped up government court suits against the railroads, which could sometimes take as long as

This locomotive was used in the logging areas of the Pacific Northwest in 1895. Special gears were developed to help the train cope with the mud, water, and rough terrain. A cylinder on each side of its frame, mounted at a 40-degree angle to the track, drove a crankshaft under the boiler that provided extra power for taking heavy loads around tight curves.

four years. In 1906, the Interstate Commerce Commission was delegated full power to establish fair and reasonable maximum railroad rates by the Hepburn Act, a major milestone in regulatory legislation.

Significant improvements in equipment were being made while the country grappled with the railroads' excesses. Major inventions included the automatic coupler, the air brake, and the railroad signal. The brakeman's job was complicated and dangerous, and the process urgently needed improvement. Turning a separate hand wheel in each car while the train moved was tricky at best. But the link and pin coupler, which required the brakeman to stand between cars, guide the link into the socket, then drop the pin, was positively hazardous. Many brakemen lost fingers in the process. After the Civil War, a Confederate veteran, Major Eli H. Janney, patented an automatic coupler in 1868. A year later, George Westinghouse patented the air brake and, in 1872, added a triple valve that supplied air pressure to each car.

The automatic coupler basically worked like the hooked fingers of two hands. With the air brakes, pipes led to each train from a tank of compressed air under the locomotive. Valves opened up as the brake handle was turned in the locomotive, allowing the air through the pipes to the brakes in each car. Both inventions worked effectively, but few railroads commissioned them. Railroad managers ruthlessly reasoned that despite injuries, labor was far cheaper than paying for these costly inventions.

The efforts of Iowa educator Lorenzo S. Coffin helped change this attitude, and these inventions became standard railroad equipment by the end of the century. Coffin lobbied widely for railroad safety reform, including Iowa legislation that required automatic couplers

CATTLE MEN READ THIS!
Great Inducements to those who wish to
Ship Cattle on the U. P. Railroad!!

Having entered into special arrangements with the **U. P. R. R.** Company, by which I can ship Cattle East at greatly reduced rates, and having selected a **point** between Carter and Church Buttes Stations some ten miles East of the former place, near the junction of the Big and Little Muddies, and having Constructed Commodious Lots and Extensive Enclosures, and the Company having put in a Switch capable of holding 40 Cars, I will be Prepared to Commence Shipping on or before the 15th of the Present Month, and will be able to promptly ship any Number of cattle that may be Offered.

Persons driving Cattle from Montana and Idaho, and passing by Soda Springs and the Bear Lake Settlements, will cross over from Bear River to the head of Little Muddy and follow down that stream, over a good road, to within a mile and a half of the junction of the Little with the Big Muddy, where they will cross a bridge and find a rich pasture, extending many miles; good water & perfect security for their stock, within convenient distance of the stock yards.

The cattle yards are in an enclosure of some 400 acres, and stock scales and all conveniences for shipping will be furnished. If parties do not wish to ship themselves, I will purchase, at good prices, all shipping cattle that may be offered. As cattle are now bearing excellent prices East, it would be well for persons to bring their Cattle forward as soon as possible.
For further particulars, address
W. A. CARTER,
Fort Bridger, Wyo. Ter.
Fort Bridger, July 2, 1877.
From W. G. Jay Clerk, Operating Orden, Utah.

A Union Pacific advertisement by a Wyoming man offering pastureland to cattlemen at a waypoint if they would use the line to ship their livestock to slaughterhouses. The joining of the Union and Pacific railroads in 1869 impacted mightily on the development of cattle and sheep ranches and wheat farms in the Midwest. By 1886, Wyoming had 8 million cattle and a half million sheep.

and air brakes on its trains, which passed by the end of the 1880s. By 1893, the Railroad Safety Appliance Act made it law that all trains nationwide be equipped with these devices.

A manual block-signal system was developed in 1865. Before the invention of this safety device, accidents often occurred when one train overtook another. With this system, no train could enter a block of space until the train in front vacated that block. The block system

The *General*, a Civil War–era locomotive, sitting before a locomotive built in 1910, illustrating the enormous increase in size and power of rail transport in a relatively short period of time.

was improved further in 1871, when it was centrally controlled and a closed electric circuit set the signals.

During this time, there were also efforts to standardize track size. Standard gauge—4 feet 8 ½ inches wide—was used in completing the Pacific railroads. The Erie, which was finished in 1880, had also laid standard-gauge tracks. But by that year, 20 percent of the nation's tracks still used nonstandard track, slowing down freight traffic. Larger gauge had been used across the mountains in the West

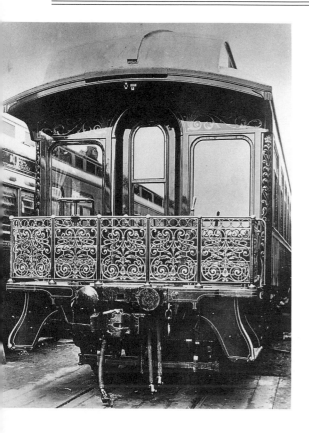

The brass-railed observation platform at the rear of Pullman's 1889 *Golden Gate* railroad car. Pullman cars were pure luxury with velvet armchairs and divans, large picture windows with attractive curtains, and ornate stained glass ceilings.

An 1896 advertisement for the Red Cap porter service offered by the New York Central Railroad at Grand Central Terminal in New York. The first porters were ex-slaves hired by the Pullman Palace Company in Chicago in 1867. Their duties included greeting passengers, storing luggage, and making beds. Wages averaged $20 a month plus tips.

A horse-drawn trolley in front of the Plaza Hotel in New York City in 1901. America's first urban railway, the New York and Harlem Railroad started a horse trolley service on rails in 1832 that ran along the Bowery from Prince Street to Fourteenth Street. By the late 1880s, there were 15,000 horses pulling streetcars throughout the city.

and in the Old South, and this had to be changed. It was a big task, but by 1896, track standardization for all lines had been completed.

American locomotives were also increasing in power. Known as the 4-4-0, the American-type locomotive had four wheels in front, four drivers, and no wheels under the cab. Heavier locomotives with more and smaller driving wheels were being used by the late 19th century, and by 1890, ten-wheeler engines pulled passenger cars weighing up to 50 tons. The Consolidation, a 2-8-0 engine that achieved more traction and pulled more freight, could pull 75 to 80 tons. Larger fireboxes were necessary to fuel these powerful locomotives, and these were developed in the 1890s. The firebox was made bigger and relocated from the rear drivers to a trailing truck. The *Pacific* locomotive, which ran for the first time on the Missouri Pacific Railroad in 1892, had 2,200 horsepower and pulled 93 tons.

While trains were becoming more powerful and efficient, passengers were enjoying luxurious interiors, thanks to George Pullman, whose distinctive cars featured hand-carved woodwork, lush carpets, and beautiful mirrors. Ever the showman, Pullman ran a transcontinental round trip from Boston to San Francisco with eight of his special cars in 1870. He manufactured hundreds of sleeping, dining, and parlor cars in the following years in the town of Pullman, right outside Chicago. In 1887, Pullman superintendent H. H. Sessions designed the vestibule, a flexible, covered passageway between cars that improved passenger safety by replacing the rickety, open platforms passengers had to cross to get from car to car.

City rail transport was evolving as well. At first, horsewagons, which pulled one or more passenger cars, wheeled around urban areas on tracks. By the mid-1880s, nearly 100,000 horses and mules pulled 18,000 cars for various railway companies. But these cars were

The intersection of Fifth and Walnut streets in Cincinnati in 1893.

Hitching a ride on an electric trolley. Electrified railways eventually replaced horse-drawn trolleys.

Margaret O'Leary, the first woman conductor on the Broadway Streetcar Line in New York City, photographed in 1917.

An early elevated subway line in New York City. Cities began looking for ways to ease congestion early in the 19th century. Plans for elevated railroads were discussed in New York as early as 1825, but the first line, the Sixth Avenue "El," did not begin trial runs until 1868.

slow and inadequate for transporting the burgeoning city populations.

In 1888, an electrified 12-mile streetcar line in Richmond, Virginia, successfully made its debut. Developed by Frank Julian Sprague, a former assistant of Thomas Edison, the new trolley streetcar had a pole located on its roof with a wheel at the end. The wheel ran along overhead wires carrying a 600-volt direct current.

By the following year, the number of interurban lines mushroomed. Two hundred trolleys were in operation or being built, 90 percent of them based on Sprague's patent or plans. These interurban electric cars filled a need that railroads could not, providing for more stops in small towns as well as places in the countryside. As a result, the Midwest had the biggest

This colorful poster announces the grand opening of the transcontinental railroad on May 10, 1869. Irish, German, and Scandinavian immigrants, former slaves, convicts, and war veterans laid the westbound tracks of the Union Pacific, and 15,000 Chinese helped to lay the eastbound tracks of the Central Pacific through the treacherous, snow-covered Sierra Nevada. The joining of the two railroads at Promontory, Utah, was cause for public celebrations throughout the United States.

concentration of these trolley systems, followed by the West Coast. Sprague, who started the Sprague Electric Railway and Motor Company, also developed a multiple-unit control that enabled several self-propelled cars to be hooked up and operated by a single set of controls that would be used by railroad companies in later years.

As cities continued to grow and expand into the surrounding countryside, transporting masses of people became a major problem.

Boston, which had 2,600 electric streetcars by the end of the century, experienced such rush-hour gridlock that passengers complained they could arrive home faster by walking across the streetcar roofs. While an underground transit system had been proposed for New York City as early as 1864—a year after London opened its subway system—the New York State legislature rejected the plan. Boston became the first American city to open a successful subway line, in 1897. The Tremont Street line cost over $4 million and could handle up to 400 cars an hour along a two-mile route. It was later extended to 22 miles.

A New York subway quickly followed in 1900. With financial backing from August Belmont, construction began on a 15-mile line running from City Hall to Harlem. Like London's subway, it was built by using a shield—a large cylindrical tube pushed by hydraulic jacks that pummeled through the underground clay and formed deep tunnels. "City Hall to Harlem in 15 minutes" became the subway's promotional theme. It opened officially to 150,000 passengers on October 27, 1904, and the first subway theft was reported that same day—a $500 diamond pin was stolen from a passenger. The electric cars traveled at a speed of 25 miles per hour. Eventually, New York's subway became the largest in the world.

Motor Vehicles

WHILE RIDING THE RAILS WAS THE FASTEST, MOST EFFICIENT way to get to America's inland towns and villages, the railroad companies needed to be reined in. By the end of the 19th century, they had become very powerful. But soon their monopoly on transportation would be broken by a new invention.

Better roads were in great demand, but not much was done until the appearance of the bicycle. Albert A. Pope had been manufacturing high-wheeled velocipede bicycles from his Hartford, Connecticut, plant since 1878. Biking already had a following, but after the geared, low-wheeled safety bike was introduced in 1885 by J. F. Starley in Coventry, England, American bikers took to the roads in great numbers. In most cases, these enthusiasts found the roads unmarked and poorly surfaced and maintained. Not surprisingly, Pope became a major supporter of the Good Roads movement.

Highway improvement legislation eventually was passed in New Jersey in 1891, and other states soon followed. In 1893, an Office of Road Inquiry was established within the Department of Agriculture.

Photographed in 1946, Henry Ford takes a ride on the first automobile to come out of his shop on Bagley Avenue in Detroit, Michigan, in 1896. Ford grew up on a farm, but he hated plowing and planting, preferring instead to tinker with machinery. As a teenager, he encountered steam-powered farm machines that were used to thresh grain and saw wood, and he had a vision of a self-propelled vehicle that would carry people from place to place.

Charles Duryea photographed with his first horseless carriage in 1895. Charles and his brother Frank were the first Americans to build a gasoline-powered automobile in 1893. By the late 1890s, there were at least a hundred aspiring auto manufacturers looking for financial backing, and auto racing was a way to draw attention to one's invention. On Thanksgiving Day in 1895 in Chicago, the Duryeas won America's first auto race. A Duryea car ran the 52-mile course at an average speed of 6.6 miles per hour. America's first auto accident also involved a Duryea car. Henry Wells of Springfield, Massachusetts, collided with a bicycle rider.

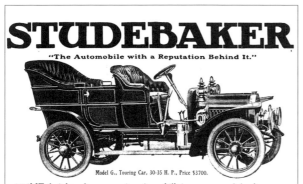

STUDEBAKER

"The Automobile with a Reputation Behind It."

Model G., Touring Car, 30-35 H. P., Price $3700.

THE height of sane engineering skill is represented in the new Studebaker models. For high efficiency with low weight; for progressiveness tempered with common sense; for elegance combined with durability; for noiseless mechanism; for ease of control; for accessibility of vital parts—for "cars built for service," look to Studebaker.

Three Gasoline Models		Six Electric Models	
Model E, 20-24 H. P. - - $2600.		**Model 22,** Runabout - - $1050.	
4-cylinder, storage battery, jump spark ignition.		**Model 24,** Stanhope - - $1200.	
Model F, 28-32 H. P. - - $3000.		**Model 16,** Victoria-Phaeton - $1750.	
4-cylinder, storage battery, jump spark ignition.		**Model 20,** Surrey - - $2800.	
Model G, 30-35 H. P. - - $3700.		**Model 21,** Station Wagon - $3500.	
4-cylinder, Sims-Bosch low tension, magneto ignition.		**Model 2012,** 14-Passenger Omnibus $2800.	

Also five models of automobile trucks and delivery wagons.
Complete catalogues on application.

Studebaker Automobile Co.
South Bend, Ind.

Members Association of Licensed Automobile Manufacturers.

Studebaker Repositories.

NEW YORK CITY - - Broadway and 48th Sts.
CHICAGO, ILL. - - 378-388 Wabash Ave.
SAN FRANCISCO, CAL. - Cor. Market and 10th Sts.
KANSAS CITY, MO. - - 13th and Hickory Sts.
PORTLAND, ORE. - - 330-336 E. Morrison St.
SALT LAKE CITY, UTAH - 157-159 State St.
DENVER, COLO. - - Cor. Fifteenth and Blake Sts.
DALLAS, TEX. - - 317-319 Elm St.

Selling Agencies.

ALTOONA, PA., W. H. & L. C. WOLFE, 1011 Chestnut Ave.
BOSTON, MASS., HARRY FOSDICK CO., 53-55 Stanhope St.
BUFFALO, N. Y., NATIONAL BATTERY CO.
CLEVELAND, OHIO, CENTRAL AUTOMOBILE CO., 409 Erie St.
CINCINNATI, OHIO, HANAUER AUTOMOBILE CO., 118 E. 7th St.
ERIE, PA., C.R.DENCH, ERIE FIREPROOF GARAGE, 12th & State Sts.
PHILADELPHIA, PA., TITMAN, LEEDS & CO., 1277 Market St.
PITTSBURG, PA., BANKER BROS. CO., Baum and Beatty Sts.
LOS ANGELES, CAL., W.G. NEVIN, Hellman Bldg., Cor. 4th and Spring Sts.
WASHINGTON, D. C., NATIONAL AUTOMOBILE CO., 1,11-13 14th St., N. W.

Studebaker was originally known for wagon making. This advertisement offers nine different models of automobiles, three powered by gasoline engines and six by electricity.

Eleven years later, although most of the country's 2,151,570 miles of highway were dirt roads, the agency reported that seven percent had been resurfaced.

While biking helped the push for improved roads, it also laid the groundwork for the auto industry. Many of the technologies used in bike manufacturing were later adapted to make cars. Tubular steel framing, ball and roller bearings, variable speed transmissions, and most important, the pneumatic tire, were all bicycle innovations used in auto manufacturing.

The freedom that the bike offered furthered the dream of a horseless carriage. Prototypes had been developed as far back as 1769, when a French artillery officer, Nicolas-Joseph Cugnot, built a self-propelled, three-wheeled, steam-powered vehicle that went over 2 miles per hour. In the 1890s, an internal-combustion engine powered by coal tar had been developed. Inventors were trying to decide what type of fuel would successfully power a self-propelled vehicle. It was the gasoline engine, invented in Germany by Carl Benz and Gottlieb Daimler in 1885, that provided the answer.

Benz was responsible for spark ignition. Daimler reasoned that an internal-combustion engine had to operate at high speed to generate power, and he designed and built a two-cylinder engine that produced 1.5 horsepower at 600 rpm. Benz and Daimler grasped the intricate technology that made the gasoline car work. Daimler's engine was used, under license in France by Armand Peugeot and the woodworking firm of Panhard and Levassor, in constructing cars to be sold commercially by the end of the decade. They named their new products automobiles.

Charles and Frank Duryea were the first Americans to build a successful gasoline automobile, in 1893. The Springfield, Massachusetts, inventors got their ideas from a *Scientific American* article describing Benz's car, and they put their mechanical background to work. They produced 13 cars over a five-year period with funding from Springfield businessmen.

Albert Pope, already the largest bicycle manufacturer in the country, became the first auto manufacturer in 1895. His plant built electric and gasoline cars in Hartford, and his business eventually

(continued on page 73)

A streetcar motorman in New York City in the early 1900s. Horses were taken off the trolley lines when streetcars converted to electric power in 1901.

Many illustrators satirized the mechanical weaknesses of early automobiles. Tires usually wore out after only 1,500 miles, and changing them was a chore.

A young couple pictured during a tender moment sitting in an automobile. Even the first cars, with all their mechanical problems, offered people an unaccustomed freedom and privacy.

A painting of Wilbur Wright demonstrating his *Flyer* over the French countryside. On a visit to Le Mans, France, Wilbur kept his machine in the air for 2 hours 18 minutes, covering a distance of 77 miles and winning a $4,000 prize.

(*continued from page 68*)

spread to four manufacturing locations. The company, however, went out of business by 1910.

While there were several American pioneer automobile inventors who cropped up after the Duryea brothers, Henry Ford and Alexander Winton were the only two who forged great or at least stable companies lasting a quarter century and more. Winton, a major bicycle manufacturer in Cleveland, Ohio, who founded the Winton Motor Carriage Company, became the leading producer of gasoline cars right after the turn of the century. His production was not large-scale, but he operated successfully for 25 years.

Henry Ford was the visionary who revolutionized the auto industry. Ford, initially an engineer who kept the engines running at the Edison Illuminating Company in Detroit, had always been an innovator. As a child growing up on his family farm in Michigan, he cajoled friends into building a dam behind their school, as well as a steam engine that eventually blew up. He even invented a device that allowed a wagon driver to open a gate without leaving his vehicle. Ford was drawn to machines like a magnet, even though his father encouraged him to pursue farming.

Ford had already completed building his first gasoline engine at home in 1893. His lab was a brick shed behind his house, where he experimented late at night after his day job with Edison. It took him about two and a half years, but on June 4, 1896, Ford finished construction of his first car and made a successful test run on his neighborhood streets during the early morning hours. He was the fifth American to successfully produce an experimental gasoline automobile.

Motor vehicles were appearing more frequently by the turn of the century. The U.S. Post Office started using motorized transportation

The 1901 De Dion motor carriage, built by France's Count Albert De Dion. Early American cars benefited from the technological innovations of European individuals like De Dion and Gottlieb Daimler and Karl Benz in Germany.

as early as 1896. New Yorkers were riding in electric cabs, and eastern city department stores were commissioning trucks for deliveries. Motor-driven ambulances appeared in 1900, and by 1903, in some cities fire fighters were using motorized fire trucks.

Rain aprons for daring motorists, 1904.

A 1904 advertisement for rain aprons for passengers of open touring cars. Jumping into the family car and going for a spin was not an easy thing to do in the early days of the automobile. In the country it was difficult to find garages and there was no way of letting anyone know that your car had broken down. Before driving away, motorists went through a checklist—goggles, tow rope, tire pump and tire patches, extra rim lugs, a block and tackle or winch, extra cans of gasoline and oil, a spotlight, a compass, tire chains, a jack and wooden planks to support it, and a canvas bucket. Stores like Hammacher Schlemmer & Company sold a hefty Tourist Auto Kit that weighed 18 pounds.

Ford quit his engineering job at Edison to work on his invention full-time and seek financial backing. After a couple of false starts, he formed the Ford Motor Company in Detroit in 1903. His first car, the Model A, had an 8-horsepower engine and a transmission with two forward gears and reverse. It accelerated to 30 miles per hour and

The replica at Greenfield Village of the Bagley Avenue shed in Detroit where Henry Ford built his first automobile. When the car was ready, Ford found that it was too large to fit through the door of the shed, and part of the adjoining wall had to be knocked down to get the vehicle out.

In 1917, Joseph Crichrion of Monterey, California, invented this bizarre pedestrian shield to gently push people out of the way of the automobile. By 1916, with more than three million autos on the road, the battle between pedestrians and drivers had already begun.

78

This 1827 velocipede was typical of many of the bicycle designs of the times. Riders used their feet to push backward against the ground. The handle fixed to the front axle was the steering mechanism. By 1879, Harry Lawson had designed a "safety bicycle" with pedals operating a chain linked to the rear axle and brakes that worked by pedaling backward. Early bikes were "boneshakers" with their iron or wooden wheels rolling over cobblestone streets. In the 1880s, John Dunlop of Ireland developed an inflatable pneumatic tire that made riding much more comfortable.

was surprisingly nimble on the country's less-than-perfect roads. The Model A of 1906 cost $750 and the Ford Motor Company produced 15 cars daily. It also provided customer service through its dealers, something no one else was doing.

There were several auto companies operating with the same intensity as Ford. The Olds Motor Works, founded by Ransom Eli Olds, had an annual production of 5,000 cars in 1904 and was one of

This 1886 tricycle had gears for varying speed and pedal effort, like modern bicycles.

Ford's major competitors. But Ford's major contributions—the mass production of an affordable car called the Model T and the establishment of the assembly line system of production—were what set him apart.

Others produced affordable cars, but their durability was questionable. Ever on the lookout to improve his models, Ford wanted to make a strong, sturdy, lightweight vehicle that could easily be fixed by the owner. Ford found his answer as he scavenged

A hand-cranked bicycle produced in 1869. By 1900, there were 10 million bicycles in the country.

A bicycle built for two, circa 1886. These high-wheelers were not easy to mount. The modern tandem bicycle was perfected by 1893.

through the engine parts of a French car that had crashed during an auto race in Palm Beach, Florida. A tough but lightweight valve he had retrieved was sent out for analysis. It was made of steel as well as a rare metal called vanadium, which was available only in Europe.

Ford sought out a British metallurgist and brought him to the States so that a small Ohio steel company, which had been promised future orders from Ford, could learn how to make the vanadium steel alloy. The Model T made its debut in 1908. It was the first auto with parts made of vanadium steel.

The Model T had a four-cylinder engine, could accelerate to 45 miles per hour, and got 20 miles to the gallon. Its new ignition system used magnets instead of dry-cell batteries to spark the cylinders. It tackled steep hills and sand with ease, thanks to its gears. And repairs could be made with simple tools.

Ten thousand Model Ts were sold in its first year. The car cost $1,000. Obviously, Ford could sell more if the price were below $600. But to accomplish this, production costs had to be reduced. With the Model A, workers brought parts for assembly to the chassis, which was stationed in one spot on the factory floor. It took 20 minutes to assemble one component under this system. Production chief Charles Sorensen suggested a moving assembly line; Ford hired someone to develop the idea. Ford needed a bigger factory and moved to his new Detroit headquarters in 1910. In the original test run of his assembly system, chassis were pulled through by rope. With the assembly line, one man was responsible for a single repetitive operation; the worker stayed in place as the car and the parts came to him. A subassembly could now be put together in four minutes. The assembly time for an entire Model T went from from 12 hours to 93 minutes.

Production of Model Ts soared from 78,000 in 1912 to 248,000 in 1914, when the assembly line became fully operational. Ford had accomplished what he had set out to do and dropped his price from $600 in 1912 to $490 by 1914, passing along the savings in production costs to the customer. There were 5 million cars on the nation's roads by 1917. Every other one was a Ford.

Air Transportation

IN 1885, WHEN THE MODERN TWO-WHEELED SAFETY BIKE became popular, two brothers named Wilbur and Orville Wright took to the roads and joined the cycling craze. They had been handy at tinkering when they were young, building kites and a special machine that folded newspapers, so it was not surprising that they excelled at repairing bikes. They started the Wright Cycle Company in 1892 in Dayton, Ohio, and their shop on West Dayton offered bicycle sales, rentals, and repairs. Just as Ford's brick shed served as his lab for the Model A, by 1899, the Wright brothers were working intently in a back room of the bike shop, developing an invention called an airplane.

The idea of flight had been around since the Renaissance period, when the Italian artist Leonardo da Vinci drew designs of artificial wings and helicopters, but the idea did not become tangible until the 19th century. Sir George Cayley of Great Britain championed heavier-than-air flight and designed a fixed-wing engineless aircraft in 1809.

Professor C. E. Ritchell in his flying balloon over Hartford, Connecticut, in 1878. Jacques-Étienne and Joseph-Michel Montgolfier of France built large balloons of paper and silk lifted by hot air, but the first man to ascend in a balloon was Jean-François Pilàtre de Rozier in 1783.

Initial experiments were mostly with gliders and balloons. The first successful flight in a powered machine took place in Paris, France, in 1852 when Henri Giffard flew an aerial steamship with a 3-horsepower steam engine. It traveled 17 miles, but the airship could only go 5 or 6 miles per hour, and the slightest breeze would have overcome its ability to make headway. An Austrian named Paul Haenlein tested an airship powered by a gasoline engine in 1872 in Brno, Moravia, that attained a speed of 9 miles per hour.

Other airship models were introduced, including one powered by a one-man bicycle, which was tested in Hartford, Connecticut, in 1878. In 1881, an electrically propelled version was constructed by Albert and Gaston Tissandier in Paris, France. A ripping panel allowed the gas to escape from these nonrigid airships so that they could deflate themselves immediately. The rigid airship, introduced in 1897, had to be brought down slowly and carefully, which made it difficult to land in bad weather.

A German named Otto Lilienthal inspired the Wright brothers to study the aerodynamics of flight. Lilienthal built several versions of a glider in the 1890s and made close to 2,000 unpowered flights before falling to his death. Interested in any information he could gather on flight, Wilbur Wright contacted the Smithsonian Institution.

Samuel Pierpont Langley, a prominent scientist and head of the Smithsonian, had been building and testing model airplanes since 1887. His biggest successes were the launches of two model airplanes in 1896 that soared long enough to impress the U.S. Army, which gave $50,000 toward his experiments. Octave Chanute, another American, had visited Otto Lilienthal in Germany and conducted his own gliding experiments. Lilienthal and Chanute concluded that an aircraft's wings should be curved. The curved wing, convex on top

An airship at the St. Louis Exposition in 1904. Germany became the leader in airship design, and most large airships built over the next 40 years had the rigid metal frame holding gas bags filled with hydrogen as perfected by the Germans.

and concave underneath, produced reduced air pressure above the wing and increased air pressure below it, providing the lift. Both men published books about their theories and experiences, which the Wright brothers read; later, the Wrights would seek their advice.

The Wright brothers made history because of their success in controlling their aircraft once it flew, something everyone else had struggled with. They found the key by twisting the wings' tips to maintain lateral balance, just as birds alter the shape of their wings to change direction during flight. They tried this technique on a kite first, and then on a full-size glider.

Their testing site was a village called Kitty Hawk, North Carolina, on the Atlantic coast, where winds regularly reached from 10 to 20 miles per hour. The Wrights selected this area in 1900 from a list of the windiest Weather Bureau stations in the country, and its sandy beach was perfect for low-impact landings. Its remoteness also afforded the inventors almost total privacy.

The Wrights worked tirelessly after hours in their bike shop in Dayton, testing airfoil sections in a homebuilt wind tunnel. Because existing internal-combustion engines were too heavy, the Wrights designed their own motor. Their four-cylinder, fuel-injected, water-cooled engine weighed only 200 pounds.

On the cold, blustery morning of December 17, 1903, four and a half years after Wilbur Wright's first letter to the Smithsonian, the Wrights' plane, the *Flyer*, made a successful, historic flight at Kitty Hawk. The *Flyer* soared for 12 seconds and traveled a distance of 120 feet on its first trip. Orville, who piloted the aircraft, described the flight's significance as "the first in the history of the world in which a machine carrying a man had raised itself by its own power into the air in full flight, had sailed forward without reduction of speed, and had finally landed at a point as high as that from which it had started." The aircraft, built with ingenuity and resourcefulness, cost the Wrights about $1,000 in materials and parts.

The Wrights realized their invention had to remain in the air for longer periods of time if it was to be taken seriously. They built several more aircraft, moving their experimental airstrip from Kitty Hawk to a field called Huffman Pasture on the outskirts of Dayton. By 1905, the Wright *Flyer No. 3* could remain in the air as long as there was fuel and had achieved a flight lasting 39 minutes. The simple biplane, with twin propellers in the rear, could take off, maneuver in the air, and land while carrying two people in an upright position.

The Wrights applied for patents and offered their plane to the U.S. War Department. The army was hesitant; it had invested substantial funds in Samuel Langley's model airplane experiments, which had proved disappointing. But a turning point came for the Wrights when they took their *Flyer* to France in 1907, anticipating possible trials for the French government or the interest of a private syndicate that might want manufacturing rights. Wilbur was a sensation at Le Mans during a public demonstration in August 1908. Back home, Orville flew a test plane in September at Fort Myer, Virginia, that satisfactorily passed army specifications for its newly formed Aeronautical Division. In 1909, the army paid $30,000 for the Wrights' latest design, and the American Wright Company was founded in Dayton.

By 1910, air shows were a major form of entertainment in America. Aviators flew in exhibition teams or alone, their goal to break altitude and speed records for cash. Huge crowds would gather to watch these "barnstormers." One of the first major American air shows, in

Orville Wright's glider, photographed in 1908. The Wright brothers conducted experiments and meticulously studied aerodynamic principles for seven years before they achieved powered flight.

Los Angeles, featured grandstands built to accommodate 25,000 people. Ten thousand spectators turned out just to watch the country's first airmail delivery on September 24, 1911, when 1,900 letters and postcards were picked up at Nassau Boulevard in Mineola, New York, and deposited three miles away.

The Wright brothers' first powered flight, photographed on December 17, 1903, by one of their assistants. Orville is the pilot, Wilbur stands to the right.

A local Norfolk, Virginia, newspaper reported on the first flights at Kitty Hawk on December 18, 1903.

In 1911, the Goodyear Tire and Rubber Company produced the first American-made semirigid airship, a 285-foot-long aircraft called the *Akron*. The *Akron* was made of a unique fabric called rubber, invented by a Scottish company that granted Goodyear American rights. The *Akron* exploded 15 minutes into its demonstration flight from Atlantic City, but Goodyear would eventually become America's leading airship manufacturer.

The Wrights had done some early experiments with hydroplanes, but it was Glenn Curtiss who in 1912 developed a flying boat with a single pusher propeller and an engine mounted below the upper

While the Wright brothers proved that a heavier-than-air machine could fly, the next step was to develop a practical flier that could stay in the air longer than a few seconds. By 1909 they had accomplished that goal. Here Wilbur Wright confidently flies over the Hudson River near New York City.

wing. Curtiss, an aviation enthusiast from upstate New York, headed a small team organized by Alexander Graham Bell, inventor of the telephone, in an effort to develop a flying machine. Curtiss invented the aileron, a movable flap at the trailing edge of the wing that performed the same function as the Wrights' wing warping, making it possible to turn the airplane. Curtiss would be locked in a patent infringement suit with the Wright brothers for several years over the aileron, which the Wrights felt was too similar to their own method of warping the wing. But Curtiss's planes won trophies, and he was responsible for the compact pusher biplane that set many records.

Meanwhile, the War Department was proving to be very conservative on aircraft expenditures; only $250,000 had been spent between 1908 and 1913, while European countries with aircraft labs were spending millions. Italy was the first country to use the airplane during a war, in its campaign against Turkey during 1911 and 1912. Captain Carlo Piazza flew the first officially recorded reconnaissance flight over enemy lines on October 23, 1911.

Foreign powers initially thought of the airplane as a reconnaissance tool, but pilots were soon dropping bombs from their cockpits. Second Lieutenant Giulio Gavotti dropped the first bombs on a Turkish position in 1911. By the time World War I broke out in 1914, France was leading the world in aircraft construction, licensed aviators, and flight records. By 1918, Germany was using large formations of airplanes in its offensive, and Britain lost over a thousand planes during two months of fighting.

Glenn Martin, an aviator famous for his exhibition flying, started up a sizable aircraft manufacturing operation in Los Angeles in 1912. By 1913, he had developed an armored biplane and was designing a

The interior of the Wrights' workshop in Dayton, Ohio, photographed in 1910. In 1912, Wilbur Wright was killed in a crash. In 1915, Orville sold his business to Wall Street investors, though he was kept on by the new owners at a respectable salary to attract stock purchasers.

knapsack parachute. His Martin TT Tractor had a tight steel body that absorbed engine vibrations, resulting in more comfortable flights for pilots and better aiming stability for guns.

The TT Tractor became one of several aircraft reviewed by the new aviation section of the Signal Corps, which had been formed in 1914 because of the war in Europe. The army was hurrying to establish guidelines for building an air force from the sketchy information it could glean from abroad. In 1917, the navy ordered nine experimental nonrigid airships from Goodyear. In that same year, there were seven American combat squadrons; four in the United States, two in Panama, and one in the Philippines. By the end of 1918, $100 million had been invested in developing American warplanes, but the planes that were to be built in this country to help the European allies did not arrive on time.

America, which had started as a leading pioneer in aviation, failed miserably in its contribution to World War I aviation technology because of government inexperience and mismanagement and corporate profiteering. When the government established the Aircraft Production Board, it was made up mostly of automobile manufacturers who had little knowledge of aviation. Some of the largest government contracts were given to new companies, funded by auto interests, that had never made planes before.

FURTHER READING

Bailyn, Bernard, et al. *Great Republic: A History of the American People.* 3rd ed., vol. 2. Lexington, MA: Heath, 1985.

Biddle, Wayne. *Barons of the Sky.* New York: Holt, 1991.

Braynard, Frank O., and William H. Miller. *Fifty Famous Liners.* New York: Norton, 1982.

Caffrey, Kate. *The Mayflower.* Briarcliff Manor, NY: Stein and Day, 1974.

Carse, Robert. *Ports of Call.* New York: Scribners, 1967.

Cavin, Ruth. *Trolleys: Riding and Remembering the Electric Interurban Railways.* New York: Hawthorn Books, 1976.

Chappelle, Howard I. *American Small Sailing Craft.* New York: Norton, 1951.

The Chronicle of America. Mount Kisco, NY: Chronicle Publications, 1989.

INDEX

Picture Credits

The Bettmann Archive: pp. 10, 11, 12, 13, 15, 16, 19, 20–21, 24, 28, 30, 33, 35, 36, 37, 38, 41, 43, 46, 47, 49, 50, 51, 52, 54, 56, 57, 58 (right), 59, 60, 61 (top), 62, 63, 66, 69, 70, 71, 72, 75, 76–77, 80, 81, 82, 86, 88, 91, 93, 94, 96; Library of Congress: pp. 32 (neg. #LCD4-19395), 74 (neg. #LC USZ62-19497), 79 (neg. #LC USZ62-39733), 92 (neg. #LC USZ62-6166A); Smithsonian Institution: p. 23; UPI/Bettmann: pp. 34, 39, 58 (left), 61 (bottom), 78.

LINDA LEUZZI is an author and journalist whose work has been featured in New York *Newsday, Family Circle, Ladies' Home Journal, Weight Watchers, New Woman,* and *The Norton Environmental Reader,* a college textbook. She is a consultant for the Science Museum of Long Island, an interactive science activity center for children and adults in Plandome, New York.